CW00505237

Acknowledgements:

Acknowledgements are due to the editors of the following publications, in which some of these poems first appeared: *The Moth* (Spring 2012) for 'mark'; *Small Candles* (2012) for 'the shirt'; *South* No. 52 (2015) for 'the truth is there between us'; *More Points on the Compass* (2017) for '71B', 'bamboo', 'the crows' and 'the wedding'; *Strix 1* (2017) for 'the death of poetry' and 'before'; *About Larkin 44* (2017) for 'tadpoles'; *Strix 5* (2018) for 'the pillbox'.

A number of other poems from this collection will appear in anthologies scheduled to be published in 2020: 'the porpoises' and 'the shirt' are due to appear in *Hull City of Poets*; 'dragonflies' and 'further' are due to appear in an anthology of poems written at Linley Hill.

For their support, suggestions and advice many thanks to Andy Fletcher, Joanne McMillan, Ann McCollum, Jim Orwin, John Osborne, Tony Petch, Beate Swoboda, Marianne Vagle, Bruce Woodcock, Mutiny Writers and the Hull and Rural Yorkshire Stanza groups.

living by the law of light

First published in 2019 by dancing sisters

This collection © 2019Mary McCollum

d a n c i n g s i s t e r s . c o . u k

ISBN 978-1-9997071-4-9

ISBN 978-1-9997071-5-6 (ebook)

MARY McCOLLUM

living by the law of light

DANCING SISTERS

HULL

2019

CONTENTS

for Mum and Dad

beginning

a grove of red sumac

flames lick the air
above a bed of leaves
where desire survives
with the fire of a first time

i am the world i see

first light

to wake up is sometimes a going under
returning
unsure of what's a dream and what's real

i remember running across an open field

there's a before to everything when it's pure

shining rings begin
when a leaf falls on water

night train

in the distance
across dark fields
greenhouses are lit up

from the window of the train
they're a city of light

a promise

the horizon's invisible
the land indivisible from
the black dome of the sky

filtered through a passenger's earphones
the faint din of a song

the discomfort of hope

urgency and eternity meeting
on the night train home

where does a poem come from?

how is it received?

the luminous greenhouses
disappearing into the night

the beach

the beach is a great leveller

we're all happy peasants here

it's impossible to feel important
with the tide stealing even your footprints

we should make our leaders meet here
to stop them locking themselves
in towers of reflective glass
to decide our future

they could hold all their summits on the beach
wear swimming costumes and hawaiian shirts
sit on towels and get sand in uncomfortable places

they could have regular breaks
to stroll along the shore hand in hand
throw balls for dogs
play frisbee
and make sandcastles with children

that'd keep them grounded

all their agreements would be written on the sand
for the next tide to wash away
leaving scores of upturned shells
strewn like the hats of chinese peasants
who'd thrown a hurrah into the air

lucy

'do you want the good news or the bad?'

it's lucy
ringing from belfast
10.30 at night
i can picture her
with a cigarette and glass of wine

i choose 'good news'
'i'm getting married' she says

it's been a few months since i saw her
i didn't even know she had a boyfriend
'congratulations' i say 'and...?'
'i'm dying' she says 'got six months'

i don't know why i wait so long
but i fly to belfast three weeks later

opening the door to me
lucy says 'do you not do death?'
and 'hope you brought a bottle of champagne'

by now she can barely swallow anything
so i drink most of the bottle

the next time i see lucy is at her wedding

when she and her new husband kieran
take the floor for the first dance
the rest of us gather in a circle
as if we can hold them
hold onto them

the dj plays the undertones' 'teenage kicks'
and we kick up our legs
against sorrow
against death

three weeks later
lucy's name lights up on my mobile

when i answer
it's her sister cait's voice
on the other end of the line

the shirt

in my neighbour's garden a shirt
that's been left out on the washing line
all winter

weather worn how many times
has it been soaked then frozen?
this is a well established form of torture
wet then cold

i do not take it down
i could be accused of theft

i do not take it down
it is not mine

a gust of wind picks it up
it dances though the effort
is desperate
it's been violated so often

beneath the washing line grow
clumps of snowdrops
not one lifts its head
they study the ground
like guilty children
staring at their shoes

tadpoles

a tad too small
for polevaulting across the pond

do they dream of giant leaps
when they'll grow into frogs
for pale lads to pet?

doleful days in the dales

dappling rain

the plop sounds of nature

tadpoles
adept at adapting

toppling over

looping the loop

olé!

if i could turn back time

a digger outside the british extracting company
excavating the sky
and hollowing out the silent air

a teenager cycles by
on a bike that's too small for him

a sound system with speakers
is rigged up on the handlebars
and the back of the bike

the words 'if i could turn back time' blare out

suddenly i have a knot in my belly
and i'm crying
and i don't know why

irises

when the night of conversation has passed
the sunlight reminds us of the aspens
outside the window
an extraordinary bridge

cold soot in the grate. we agree
that trees a bird the open sky
are preferable to the abysmal dead
our wasted friends
a drunk girl in a flowered dress

life after an evening of such thoughts astonishes
we no longer sit or stand like stones in a museum

is death a falling through a sieve
face beaten skin a bright white velvet?

love is another word

we're alone again
with the morning sun on far off trees

the irises in the vase have opened
deranged by light

the wedding

the teeth of the saw
bite into the wood

you push i pull

our friends are willing us
to work in perfect synchronicity

i push you pull

the log dribbles sawdust

the saw protests
catches
complains on the return

you push i pull

we've an awkward rhythm
not tongue in groove
not smooth

we don't instinctively sense
when the other will change
from push to pull
or pull to push

our unevenly matched arm lengths
take some getting used to

with the log and the saw connecting us
we're jerkily discovering
what it may be like in the years to come

the second longest pier in the world

weather's not good
raining all morning

hoping it'll improve for len's birthday

ruth's taking amber to see the dolphins on tuesday

amber was stung by a wasp
but she was lucky the swelling went down pretty quickly

david's had two games of golf

hope you like the picture of the second longest pier in the world

barefoot woman

a woman's walking barefoot on a rope
strung between two trees in the park

frost on the dead leaves
covering the grass beneath her

the sun clinging onto the low bars
of the sky's climbing frame

on a wall someone's sprayed the words
maybe it's the world that's mad

the woman holds out her arms
for balance

i ask 'aren't your feet cold?'
'no' she says 'not so long as i stay on the rope'

disposable

the woman who cleans out latrines
with her bare hands is an 'untouchable'

the fund-raising leaflet tells me
35p will buy her a pair of rubber gloves

the voice

the voice is squeezing out
from under the stone
you dropped on it

the voice is remembering itself

you keep hitting it
but you can't kill it

you can't hurt the voice

you try to ignore it
but the voice tells you it's never leaving

the voice is what cracks the egg
so the chick can be born

the voice tells the fledgling
to jump from the nest

the voice is the sky
the moorland and sea

it sounds like death
it sounds like sunshine

the voice will always be here
until it's the only thing here

surface tension

lilac that's more than a word

lilac in a vase
on top of the gas heater

the purple blossom
startling against the white wall

the flowers lean into the room
as if listening
for an answer to a question
only they can hear

the boy with dark eyes

a rose and a broken vase

water spilling
finding its way through the cracks
of the scrubbed wooden table

light reflecting from the surface

the boy with dark eyes looks straight through you

the past has nothing to do with him

he lives without memory
in the rinsed bowl of the present

the tap permanently running

the grasshopper

in the field the long grass is dying in the heat

a grasshopper crosses my path

leaps once
           twice
                 and disappears
into the undergrowth

this wild place
      in the middle of the city
            has nettles as tall as me

in a fable
      a grasshopper
            instead of working like an ant
            sang all summer
then died of starvation when winter came

this afternoon we closed the leafy curtains
            in our green room
                and went to bed

our wild place

i don't believe in fables

later i walked to the field
        singing

further

you pick a sprig of meadowsweet
and give it to me

you turn back and i continue

i often don't go far enough
so today i'm walking further

a dragonfly rises ahead of me

i climb over a five-bar gate

i've never been beyond this point before

the grass is getting longer

crickets leap before my feet

by going further
i may find
what i hadn't thought of looking for

grief

pampas grass in a winter garden

fluffy heads
holding up in the freezing wind

you've been a widow three days

grief's an intruder
whose language you don't speak

you sit in silence
and watch a crow take off from a rooftop

black wings huge against the sky

mark

one day mark hoolihan called at our front door
and offered me a bottle of orange juice
nobody ever came to our front door
mark hoolihan never came to our house.
he wasn't a friend of my brothers though
he was the boy with whom two years before
i'd played *i'll show you mine*
if you show me yours

i cannot explain why with the inevitability
of a tragic hero i fell in so easily
with his plans. i'd hardly ever seen him
in our seven years but he'd materialise
to conjure seminal moments like this
the one and only time i ever drank piss

the back seat

we're in your son's jaguar

in the back seat
i see everything

the dark geometry of winter trees
the dark geometry of three-lane traffic

wind turbines
turning dusk into night

the motorway's a conveyor belt

like on a tv game show
you get to keep what you remember

the windscreen wipers are moving in time
to bruce springsteen singing 'everything's the same'

but it's not
it's never the same

what will i recall?

the mystery of lit up lorries
speeding out of the gloom?

poem

it's only from a grey sky like this
snow can fall

i'm looking at the white ground while i walk

the things that belong to winter
death
endings

when i look up
a tree fills my line of vision

a sycamore tree on a grey day with snow falling

i have to remember to breathe
remember why i'm here – no
remember i am here

it depends on the configuration
this moment
this place

i see so much
looking up at the branches
spread like blood vessels
in a human lung

remembrance day

four fighter jets pass overhead

black silhouettes
appear before their sound
that fills the air
turning the cattle in the field
into statues

the planes become insects
as they approach their base
descending and disappearing
beyond the horizon

the fields of saplings
thin stems protected by plastic
are a graveyard for all the dead
of the past century's wars

entering the village i see
the flaming trees of autumn
are a fire spreading
from house to house

bamboo

if you were bamboo
i might build a fence with your stems
and put you in my garden
for shelter from the wind

if you were bamboo
i might fashion you into a chair
and sit on your lap all day

if you were bamboo
i might make you into a bed
and sleep on you at night

if you were bamboo
i might turn into a panda and eat you

this is what love is like

i am a doll's house
my front panel's been taken off
and you can see into every room

the little people are frantic
at this exposure

they're running up and down stairs
and from room to room
closing the curtains and the doors

it's hopeless

now it's not just you who can see in
anyone can

absence

my coffee has a slightly bitter after-taste

new leaves outside the window
are such a bright green
they look artificial

there's a vase of flowers on the table

the gerbera daisy's an unnatural shade of pink
and the white carnation has a purple frill
like the hem of a dress

i look and i look

there's something
i can never work out

the petals look like pleats

i study the carnation
as i might study your face
taking in every detail

what is it i feel cut off from?

in trying to find it
i lose it
even though i know
it's always there

bonding

the day i was born
did you take me in your arms
and love me?

or did i wrap myself around you
like bindweed
white trumpets peering through the leaves?

ambition

i think i'm too important a reporter
to have to cover a children's summer scheme in west belfast

the community centre has a darts board

four boys are playing table football

there's a backyard
with a game of hopscotch chalked on the concrete

i hate these assignments
when i have to ask stupid questions
just to have something to write in tomorrow's paper

the children however are excited

one tells me they're going to visit the armagh planetarium

while i'm listening
this story is becoming front page news
as i share in the promise
of the sun the moon and stars

funeral flowers

i hear you at the door

i can tell from your voice you're drunk
and i hope you won't come in
but andy invites you

you have a tray of flowers
from your mother's coffin

after her funeral today
you decided to share them
with your neighbours
as a celebration of how far you've come

'she was a complicated person' you say
'she wasn't kind or motherly'

sitting on the floor in your black dress
and tights you look smart

you've been crying complicated tears
of grief and anger

i choose a few roses and some ferns
and put them in a vase

'it was a lovely service' you say
'my friend ian made a beautiful tribute'

you tell me your daughter's at home
and she's fine

you get up and take your tray of flowers
on to the next neighbour in the terrace
telling me again
you're celebrating how far you've come

swing

a tree

a branch

a rope
strung up by children
as a swing

a young woman
stands and stares

at where a week ago
a man hanged himself

the porpoises

'did you think we'd last this long?' you ask me
 on one of our walks by the estuary
'of course' i say

from our first kiss i knew we'd stay together
but you never seem so sure

you're always surprised by us

this is a day of surprises
the two ducks swimming backwards
carried by the current
make us laugh

i see the porpoises first and
not believing my eyes
i point to where i saw them
for you to verify the sighting

we wait such a long time
peering out over the river
scanning the surface from where i saw them
out towards the mouth of the estuary

i've no idea how long a porpoise can stay under water

it's important to me that you see them too

eventually when i've almost lost faith
the fins rise in two arcs out of the water

you take my hand in yours

in silence we watch their progress as far as we can
on their way out to sea

how i want to be

i nearly didn't pick out
the peach linen blouse
from the clearance rail in the shop

a slight flaw

an impulse

now it's drying by the open window
sleeves swaying in the breeze

a looseness
a grace

sunlight shining through the weave

fascinator

it's a quandary which word to start with

i just wanted a quickie
but now a quarrel's broken out

what would a quaker recommend?

words like 'quark' and 'kumquat' maybe?

now the words are quadrupling
i can't keep up

i settle on 'orange'
it's organic it's orgasmic

an orangutan fascinated by a gnat

i tell myself 'you're greater than this'

my pen's grating

the page is a quagmire
a dark quarry
where words are squandered

'come on!' i say to myself
pouting like an orangutan
'show some grit!'

dragonflies

walking barefoot through the grass
i'm thinking of you
my old friend

i don't know
if i'll see you again

a blue dragonfly flits
into my field of vision
and when i turn to look at it
it's gone

i'm thinking of you
then i'm not thinking of you

is that another dragonfly?

these fragile blue matchsticks
striking against all the green

i keep getting a feeling
that i was going to say something
but can't remember what

words form and disappear

i'm thinking of you
then i'm not thinking of you

nothing stays still
or waits
my old friend

the grass is prickling my feet

i'm thinking of you
then i'm not thinking of you

butterfly

a butterfly
pinned to the ground by the wind

wings ruffling
it looks as though it's trying to take off

the futility of its effort
makes me remember your short life

you were no more than a cluster of cells
yet i felt you
the little vegetarian
who made me gag at the smell of meat

who lived in my body
a part of me – but separate

i felt you

wings
beating

a butterfly
pinned to the ground by the wind

before

sun illuminates the dust
that puffs up from the pile of old blankets
when she sits on them

voices downstairs are muffled

she looks up through the skylight
and using details from her science project
imagines she's a bird
or a creature from a myth

it's thousands of years since she walked the earth
since she flew low over the rhine
since she nested in the long grass by the mudflats
living by the law of light

a time before there was a heaven

a time when people looked up
and saw only stars and sky

pink geranium

the day i move in with you
a pink geranium blooms on the windowsill

the rumble of furniture

wood scraping against wood

out with the old

a pink geranium
flowering in winter

leaves
transforming light
into eagerness to grow

stripping away accumulations

what the word 'virgin' does to a girl
full as it is of coercion and control
smelling of an old priest's bad breath
and the detergent
used to clean the wooden floor of a convent
where the colour pink is scrubbed away
and cheeks turn pale from lack of sunlight
and the fear of being touched

there it is

my vocation's here with you

we'll rarely dust
or vacuum clean
or re-arrange the furniture

a pink geranium
will remind us
how colourless the world can be

solitude

wind and cloud
and thistle seeds flying

the storm's flattened the field
behind the old white house

above the crumpled landscape
the sky splits to let light through

will i ever reach the house
under the weight of this wounded sky?

i'm always outside – preferring outside
to the damp shelter within walls

whatever danced in the final days of summer
now feels a chill

a september butterfly

a longing for stillness

in the distance a voice calls

i'm rooted here
or rather i'm scattered
where dark clouds fight against the sun

the crows

two crows start fighting
with a fierce flurry of wings
beaks jabbing
loud cawing

other crows
fly down from the trees
to break up the fight

israel's bombarding gaza
the city's been reduced to rubble
on the news there are pictures of children
with shrapnel embedded in their limbs
thousands have been killed

the rest of the world cannot or will not stop this

some minutes after the fight began
all the crows fly up into the trees

no broken wings

no deaths

the deep end

a goose flies overhead its wings heaving its body through the air. the goose is crying out as if distressed at being left behind by the flock.

when i was six years old i learnt to swim on holiday in spain. dad taught me. his hand supporting my body as i splashed and kicked. his presence allowing me to throw myself into the effort without fear. one day we went for a walk in a park. i was watching pigeons and turned round to see all my family had gone. the shock of finding myself alone. i looked round at the trees the path the lake. a man appeared and took me by the hand and helped me find my parents.

years later i'm watching a goose flying south. i remember the swimming pool and my ambition to swim alone in the deep end.

the pillbox

walking on the beach i come across a concrete pillbox

i touch the concrete
i pat the concrete

'it's alright' i say
'everything's going to be ok'

the pillbox has an air of vigilance
though it's no longer needed
as a lookout post to protect the coastline

now only holiday-makers look
through its narrow windows

i stroke the concrete
warmed by the spring sun

'it's alright' i say
'everything's going to be ok'

can i feel the tension
of the war years
of the watchmen
who dared not close their eyes through the night?

i go in and look through a window
at the waves
at the lengthy horizon

'it's alright' i whisper
'everything's going to be ok'

the triumph of art

it's pissing down

and she's smiling
the girl in the skimpy black skirt
ballet pumps and fake-fur jacket

what is it about her
about how she's dressed?

i watch her run to catch the train
and i love her for her ill-preparedness
or is it indifference?

she seems oblivious to the drenching rain

she jumps just as the doors start to close
and lunges through shouting 'fucking hell!'

women and their bicycles

on a crowded commuter train
everyone's looking at a newspaper or phone
except a young woman with pink hair
wearing cycling gear
a turquoise helmet hanging by a chin strap
from the handlebar of her bike

…..

i'm walking across the park
a girl's cycling ahead of me
carrying a two-litre carton of milk in one hand
she's standing on the pedals
and for now it's just her and her bike and the milk and the balance

…..

every morning i used to cycle
to the school where i taught english
the girls never saw me arrive because they were at prayer
but sometimes in the afternoon
i'd notice one girl at the window
watching me as i began to free wheel down the hill

thaw

it snowed in the night

now the sun's strong
and the snow's melting fast
sparkling and dripping

outside the window a water drop on a leaf
has turned blue

i watch it for a while
then notice another is yellow

i've been reading a book that tells me
i have to let go of emotional attachments
so i can love

otherwise love's just an addiction

you come in and i point out one particular drop
for you to look at too
you sit beside me and put your head next to mine to see

it's a trick of the light
an angle
lasting only a moment

the truth is there between us

we've had a disagreement
and i've been crying

i look for refuge in the laundry
and go to take the clothes off the line
you come outside too
and start gathering clothes from the other end

they've dried fast
the evening sun is hot on my arms
we move towards each other
one t-shirt
one pair of underpants at a time

we meet in the middle
warm bundles of clothes in our arms

the death of poetry

someone i've never met
was out walking on a beach
at six in the morning

seeing a deer springing along on the sand
he took out his iphone
and made a video which he later posted on facebook

his friends shared it with their friends and so on
until my friend received it and shared it
and that's how i saw it and shared it

the deer leaping on and on

a save

i only ever scored one goal in my life
it felt good but i don't care that i never did it again

i'd rather walk with you beyond the pines
watch two orange-tipped butterflies dance
as you skim stones on the water

you try different sizes and shapes
round   flat
about the size of the palm of your hand seems best

ten skips are better than a goal

from the disused quarry the sound of motorcycles
is like the distant roar from the football ground
when city scored

we lie on the white stony beach
sharing my jumper for our heads
so close i can see the pores on your nose

your eyes double and blur at this distance

i cradle your head
a football in the goalie's hands

a save

so much better than a goal

i'm holding on knowing what i've got

comet

we open a bottle of your favourite gin
and raise a glass to you

when you were dying
comet 46p/wirtanen was passing the earth
only 7.3 million miles away according to nasa

it would be visible to the human eye all month

those final days
you asked for the curtains to be left open at dusk
so you could watch for the comet
above the eastern horizon

to the end
you were determined to face facts

unafraid of what you couldn't know

the comet passed
like the consolations you refused

after the funeral your sister tells us
she'd asked you in hospital
if you were ready to meet your maker
and you'd replied 'there is no god'

we look out at the night sky
aware for a moment
of the vastness of space

we clink our glasses and say 'here's to you!'

on the pavement

a trail of small stars
glittering in the sun

other people's happiness

71b

i always ask for a forward facing seat on a train
but rarely get one
so i'm travelling backwards
looking towards the city
the family and friends i've left behind

stubbled fields
autumn trees
zoom past

the colours remind me of your hair

suddenly everything reminds me of you
freight trains
loaded with containers labelled 'china'
the fading cracking paint

i watch the world recede

a deer runs across a field
and disappears into a copse

beyond the field is a wind farm
its turbines motionless in the mist

everything's subdued by a heavy white sky

i'm glad to be subdued

inside me a light is glowing
growing with every mile
that takes me closer to my destination

it's strange to have my back
to where i'm going
but when the train stops
i'll get off and face you

blowing glass

the children turn
the bunsen burner
flames to blue
place the tips
of their glass tubes
in the flames
that gutter and
turn orange
warm as street lights
on a winter night

if you and i could talk
under the street light
where we had that kiss
in the rain
what would you say?
what would i?

only one child manages
a tiny bulb of glass

the others blow too hard
and burst the tip

if a child can find this balance
between heat and force
can't we have a conversation?

can't we find a balance?

departure

through the window of the train
the light repeats

a silver river
mirroring the sun

departure
and all that it brings
gleaming
to the surface

each minute taking me further from you

one day
our separation will be final

the light reflecting off the river
blinding

how to love

what most people can do
i can usually learn

i used this mantra to calm my nerves
when starting to drive

i passed my test

other skills i've acquired are
playing the piano and
typing at a hundred words a minute

but love's not like that

it happened without
my knowing
learning
or practising

much of the day i'm unaware of it

then i look up
and there you are